THE OFFICIAL GUIDE TO
LATIN DANCING

THE OFFICIAL GUIDE TO
LATIN DANCING

Allen Dow
with Mike Michaelson

● DOMUS BOOKS
Northbrook, Illinois

Book design and production: MacDonald Graphics
Type composition: Hagle
Production coordinator: Ruth Guest
Photography: Patrick K. Snook

THE OFFICIAL GUIDE TO LATIN DANCING
Copyright © 1980 Quality Books, Inc.
A Domus Book
Published by
Quality Books, Inc.
400 Anthony Trail
Northbrook, Illinois 60062 U.S.A.

1 2 3 4 5 6 7 8 9 10

Manufactured in the United States of America

Library of Congress Cataloging in Publication Data

Dow, Allen, 1931–
    The official guide to Latin dancing.

    Includes index.
    1. Ballroom dancing.   2. Dancing—Latin America.
I. Michaelson, Mike, 1934–   joint author.   II. Title
GV1751.D685   793.3'3   79-55240
ISBN 0-89196-067-8

CONTENTS

INTRODUCTION

Latin American dancing, with its stirring, sensuous rhythms and lively and often torrid movements, has become a firmly established part of ballroom dancing in the United States and Europe. Tracing its roots to Africa, it came out of the seedy cafes of South America and the cane fields of the Caribbean islands to find a respectable place in the fashionable salons of London, Paris and New York and, later, in big-band ballrooms and small-town dancehalls across the globe.

The samba, for example, the national dance of Brazil, arrived in Paris as early as around 1905, known as the maxixe, while the perennially-popular rumba was introduced at London's Café de Paris in 1932 by the famous French teachers the Chapouls. The hedonistic tango, the Argentine dance of the *gauchos,* arrived in Europe around 1910 and gained immediate popularity as those elegant dance demonstrators Irene and Vernon Castle taught a less-torrid version.

In the 1940s, the mambo, its name borrowed from the voodoo cult, was born in the night clubs of Havana. By the 1950s, the cha-cha, an offshoot of the mambo, was sweeping across the dance floor in European and American cities. Rounding out the Latin dancer's varied repertoire are the march-like Paso Doble, a dance that captures the proud bearing of the matador, and the merenque, the brisk, peppy dance from the Dominican Republic that is characterized by a distinctive "limp" step.

As ballroom dancing entered the decade of the 1980s, it was showing every indication of enjoying a renaissance with the return of the big bands and the staging of ballroom dancing extravaganzas. And right along with the swing, the fox trot and the waltz, dancers are rising to the lively Latin beat.

before you begin:
LATIN BASICS

From the soft and romantic rumba to the sensuous and sophisticated tango, Latin dancing offers a wide and varied repertoire of dances. The following chapters of this book will present instruction in seven of the most popular Latin dances. Detailed, step-by-step descriptions and corresponding photographs provide easy-to-follow instructions for both the man's and woman's steps. However, before you begin to tackle the basics of these dances, be sure to study the pointers on style, technique and rhythm contained in this chapter.

BASIC STYLING, CLOSED POSITION

In most cases in Latin dances the man's lead arm (hand on partner's back) should be between the small of the back and shoulders (proportionate to the partner's relative height). Therefore, the man's lead arm (his right) has the elbow slightly higher than in American and European ballroom dances. This style arm (his left) also is equally elevated.

Latin Motion is an important technique to master for use in such dances as the rumba and cha-cha. Instructions for this movement are dealt with in the following chapter.

Rumba. Rumba steps (in common with cha-cha and mambo) usually are executed by stepping toe-ball-heel, as if to press foot into floor. However, it also is acceptable to do rumba steps flat-footed. As we have noted, Latin Motion is an integral part of the styling of this dance—as it is with the cha-cha and mambo—and it is achieved basically by moving the hips in opposition to the foot that is in motion (hip being over the supporting leg). Again, refer to separate description in following chapter on Latin Motion.

Cha-cha. This dance also incorporates the use of Latin Motion and, when done other than in the closed position, arms should be used in the flamboyant fashion described in the chapter dealing with this dance. When properly executed, this dance gives the appearance of the body pressing into the floor from the hips down and away from the floor from the waist up. *Pointers:* When doing steps such as the crossover, be careful not to lean upper torso over forward foot while in the parallel position—a common tendency among beginners. Also, during chassé portion of steps, avoid the tendency to be "bouncy"—another common flaw.

Merengue. This is a lively dance that exhibits a "happy" mood within its movement and within its music. Its distinctive leg motion—a kind of "limp" step—is initiated by the rib cage and hips. (See merengue chapter for an in-depth discussion of styling and the interesting story of the supposed origin of this dance.)

Mambo. Footwork is similar to that of the cha-cha and, again, flamboyant arm styling is used in positions other than closed position. This dance also incorporates Latin Motion. The mambo (in common with the tango) requires a high degree of control as the dancer becomes more advanced.

Samba. This dance also has a unique styling, characterized by a leaning forward and back motion and by a "barrel-roll" effect with partners in a close closed position. This "barrel roll" effect is achieved as follows: man leans back as partner leans forward; then man leans left and partner leans right; then man leans forward, woman leans back, then man leans right, woman leans left; then roll is repeated. Practice this technique while standing (not dancing) in the upright position. For balance, feet should be apart on forward and back diagonals.

Tango. Styling for this dance features close body contact and contra-body motion in addition to long steps with bent (this means *more* than flexed!) knees—elements which are imperative for the correct look and feeling of this dance. The upper torso should project forward, as to have a relatively straight line from knees through hips to chest (knees do *not* project in front of upper part of body). This styling usually feels awkward to beginners. In fact, if you were to stand still in this position, you would have the feeling that you are about to fall flat on your face!

Beginning-to-intermediate dancers usually tag a tango close (see step description in tango chapter) at the end of each step. More advanced dancers learn to phrase (see definition) music and may use only one or two tango closes per phrase.

In tango, the positioning of the man's lead arm and hand varies in elevation according to the step being executed—the object being to provide the strongest possible lead, control and styling. For example, in the tango fan (see step description in tango chapter), which involves passing the woman by the man's side first in one direction, then in another, the man's lead hand lowers to the small of the back so as to more easily aid his partner to drive her hips forward, providing the look desired.

Paso Doble. This dance is unlike the other Latin dances in that it has a haughty Matador look with many steps executed in a controlled march-like fashion. This look is accomplished by a raised rib cage and the appearance of strong arms—as if partners were pushing against each other without close body contact.

DEFINITIONS

Supporting leg. Leg holding body weight.

Working leg. Leg in motion (not supporting weight).

Steps. A step simply is a change of weight; shifting weight from one foot to the other. Forward, back, side and diagonal steps are taken relative to the direction of the hips. An in-place step is one in which the foot leaves the floor and returns to its original placement (although, not in all cases returning to face the same direction).

Rhythms and timing. The term "rhythm" as used throughout this book is defined as the number of beats of music per step. Timing is the dancer's ability to coordinate his or her rhythm to the rhythm of the music.

As defined in this book, a slow step is one step to two beats of music; dancer would step on count 1, count 2 either a hold or *follow through* (see separate definition). A quick step is one step per beat; dancer would step on each beat of music. For a split step, a dancer would take two steps to one beat of music. Slow, quick or split rhythms (as opposed to steps) refer to dance elements that do not have changes of weight, such as in the close portion of the tango close where dancers draw one foot to the other into a balance position.

Phrasing. In dance, this term describes the ending of a pattern or sequence of patterns to coincide with the ending of a series of melodic notes. A phrase of music usually will consist of 32 such notes.

Chassé. Chassé rhythm is comprised of one quick and one split, count 1-and-2. In chassé steps, one foot "chases" rather than passes the other, as chassé forward right, left foot forward but *not* catching or passing right, right foot forward. Chassés may be executed in any direction.

Triplet. As defined in this book, a triplet is a rhythm of 1-and-2 (three steps to two beats of music), each foot passing the other.

Turns. Turning is done with movement rather than with steps, i.e., a turn is initiated from the upper torso—usually preceding the step on which the turn occurs—and in a constant, flowing motion rather than sporadically, allowing feet to turn on forward and back motions.

Pivot. A pivot is a swivel usually done on the ball of one foot. Initial movement is caused by the turning of the upper torso, then placing weight on the ball of the pivotal foot, continuing to turn upper torso until desired amount of pivot is achieved.

Contra-body motion. This is the turning of the upper torso in the opposite direction to the legs, e.g., if dancer's left foot is forward, left shoulder should be back. As in most good dance form, the upper torso initiates movement. This movement should be fluid—body moves, foot joins it, both portions of body end movement at the same time (or body may still have some movement when step ends).

Follow through. This is a motion allowing continuity and direction from one step to another. For example, a *forward follow through* would be one leg passing the other in a forward motion; a *back follow through* would be one leg passing the other in a backward motion; a *diagonal follow through* is to go diagonally from one point to another in a straight line; a *curved follow through* is to go from one point to another, as to describe an arc with the foot.

POSITIONS

Closed position. (See basic styling, beginning of this chapter.)

Left open position. (Also known as "conversation position.") Man's left shoulder open slightly, woman's left shoulder open slightly, with man's right arm around her waist and, usually, man's left hand holding her right hand. In tango left open position, dancers' shoulders do *not* open any more than absolutely necessary to execute step (the objective is to maintain a close body contact).

Right open position. As above, reversing shoulder motion.

Right side position. Man's right upper torso from center to right of woman's upper torso, partners facing each other.

Left side position. Exact opposite of above.

Left parallel position. Partners facing same direction with woman to the right of man (some physical contact, such as man's right hand holding partner's left hand, man's right arm around her waist, etc.).

Right parallel position. Exact opposite of above.

Apart position. No physical contact between partners, as described in chase in cha-cha and mambo chapters.

Turn out. A term that describes the action of the inside of the heel of the foot pulling forward.

LATIN MOTION

Latin Motion is an integral part of the styling used in rumba, cha-cha and mambo. In essence, it is achieved by moving the hips in opposition to the foot that is in motion.

As a rule of thumb, the leg that is in motion does *not* immediately take the majority of the weight. Most of the weight remains with the hip over the foot that did not move. Work hard at practicing and perfecting Latin Motion. It absorbs bouncy movements and gives the dancer a smooth motion. And, of course, it adds panache to your execution of these three Latin dances.

In the following series, Mark demonstrates the correct styling for Latin Motion:

Remember that Latin Motion involves not only the hips but also motion of the rib cage in opposition to the hips. The hips, rather than just moving side-to-side, roll in a forward figure 8.

Mark forward right, weight remaining on left. Note: Hip remains over supporting leg (left) as rib cage pulls right. Weight would be changed by initiating movement from hip, thus freeing left foot to step in same fashion.

Mark back right, stepping without shifting weight, hip over supporting leg (left), hip pulled right.

Side steps utilize this same technique, Mark side right, right foot free of majority of weight, hip over supporting leg (left), rib cage right.

CHAPTER 3

RUMBA

Warm, tropical nights spent dancing under the stars. Soft, romantic music accentuated by the steady beat of claves, maracas and bongo drums. These are the sentimental images that often spring to mind when one visualizes the rumba, a flowing dance that quickly becomes a favorite of beginners. Although the music has a definite Latin beat, it also is very melodic, frequently featuring lots of background strings. It is music that is easy to listen to and relaxing to dance to.

Originally, the rumba was an erotic, arousing dance that found its way from Africa to the Carribbean. A slower, more sedate version was introduced into the United States from Cuba during the late 1920s. It quickly gained popularity among ballroom dancers, with movie stars George Raft and Carole Lombard among its well-known practitioners.

Footwork in the rumba should be precise. This helps accentuate the Latin look of the dance. The rhythm for the popular medium tempo (one of three tempos, and the one we will teach in this chapter) is quick-quick-slow. The count is 1-2-3-4, with the fourth beat utilizing a curved follow through motion in which the foot does *not* touch the floor (this applies to all count-four steps described in this chapter).

In rumba, steps are taken before weight change occurs, with the hip in a rolling motion. This is part of the movement known as Latin Motion, which it is important to integrate into the dance. Latin Motion is described and illustrated in the preceding chapter.

RUMBA BASIC

Begin in closed position with feet together. Mark's right hand on Lisa's back between small of back and shoulder blades, Mark's right elbow almost parallel to floor, Mark's left elbow approximately same elevation as his right. Mark's left hand holding Lisa's right, extended somewhat to left side. Lisa's left elbow approximately on Mark's right elbow, her left hand falling where it may on Mark's right shoulder. Lisa looking at Mark or over her left hand.

COUNT 1
Mark side left, Lisa side right.

COUNT 2
Mark right together left, Lisa left together right.

COUNT 3
Mark forward left, Lisa back right.

COUNT 4
This count is used for follow through motion, Mark's right foot curving toward his left and off to side, Lisa's left foot curving back toward her right and off to side. The change of weight on the side step initiates count 1 of second half of basic, as follows:

COUNT 1
(flows from count 4 of first half of basic), Mark side right, Lisa side left.

COUNT 2
Mark left together right, Lisa right together left.

COUNT 3
Mark back right, Lisa forward left.

COUNT 4
This count is again utilized for curved follow through to side, which would begin basic sequence over.

UNDERARM TURN

The underarm turn begins with basic—counts 3-4 of last half of basic Mark raises Lisa's right arm with his left arm.

COUNT 1
Mark wraps left foot behind and around right, beginning quarter turn to left while pushing Lisa's back with his right hand, guiding her under his arm. Lisa steps forward right, under arm.

COUNT 2
Mark steps side right (thus, unwinding wrap), his right arm extending to side with bent elbow or side diagonal up for style, Lisa forward left.

COUNT 3
Mark forward left, taking partner in closed position, Lisa forward right.

COUNT 4
Curved follow through into last half of basic, as follows:

Note: Lisa circles to her right (under raised hands) on counts 1-2-3, as if to walk around the edge of a small hoop, all forward steps, turn being initiated by body motion rather than turning of feet.

COUNT 1
Mark side right, Lisa side left.

COUNT 2
Mark left together right, Lisa right together left.

COUNT 3
Mark back right, Lisa forward left.

COUNT 4
Utilize this count for curved follow through.

CUBAN WALK

Cuban Walk begins at count 3-4 of last half of basic. Mark brings Lisa's right arm down (with inward motion) with his left arm. Note: Illustration shows last step of basic, arm beginning its downward motion.

COUNT 1
Mark crosses left foot behind right (note: this is not a wrap, Mark faces same direction at this point), pushing on Lisa's back with his right hand and moving his left arm in a backward motion (the look of a matador taking his cape off to the left—Lisa plays the role of the cape!). Lisa forward right.

COUNT 2
Mark side right, Lisa forward left (both continue "bullfighter" look), Mark's right hand beginning to move up for style at end of count 2.

CUBAN WALK (Ctd.)

COUNT 3
Mark begins stepping left together right, pulling left arm forward, causing Lisa to begin pivoting left on her left foot (Note Lisa's styling of legs and feet: right knee raises in front, right foot near left leg . . . right toe down). Lisa's left arm is beginning to style out to side. Note: A more flamboyant look should be achieved by reaching arms more outward and upward than illustrated.

COUNT 3 (Ctd.)
Mark's left foot completes left together right, Lisa's right foot crossing in front of and close to her left foot on ball or right foot. Partners now in parallel position.

COUNT 4
Hold position of count 3.

Partners now do last half of basic, as follows:

COUNT 1
Mark side right, Lisa side left. Note Latin Motion: Mark's hip to left, weight primarily still on left foot, Mark's rib cage pulling right; Lisa's hip to right, weight predominantly still on right, her rib cage pulling left.

COUNT 2
Mark left together right, Lisa right together left.

COUNT 3
Mark back right, Lisa forward left.

COUNT 4
Mark beginning back follow through with left foot, Lisa beginning forward follow through with right foot.

COUNT 1
Mark begins walking back left in circle, right shoulder back. Lisa forward right in circle, left shoulder forward.

COUNT 2
Mark back right, Lisa forward left.

COUNT 3
Mark back left, Lisa forward right, both still circling and remaining in parallel position.

COUNT 4
Mark utilizes this count for back follow through, Lisa for forward follow through.

For next 6 counts Mark is traveling straight back, no turn, Lisa continuing turn for next 3 counts. At count 3, partners are facing each other.

COUNT 1
Mark back right, Lisa forward left. Mark is beginning to lead Lisa with left hand to bring her in front of him, partners to finish facing each other at count 3. Note extension of Mark's left arm, keeping Lisa at a distance at this point.

COUNT 2
Mark back left, Lisa forward right.

CUBAN WALK (Ctd.)

COUNT 3
Mark back right, Lisa forward left.

COUNT 4
Mark begins back with left foot, Lisa begins forward with right foot (follow through). Change of weight takes place on count 1, below. Note: On these three walking steps Mark is bringing Lisa to him in closed position.

COUNT 1
Mark back left, Lisa forward right, Mark's arm beginning to come down to take Lisa.

COUNT 2
Mark back right, Lisa forward left, beginning to secure closed position.

COUNT 3
Mark back left, Lisa forward right. partners now have resumed closed position.

COUNT 4
This count initiates follow through into last half of basic.

Then, partners do last half of basic.

CROSSOVER

Begin with first half of basic (illustration shows count 3 of first half of basic).

COUNT 3
Mark forward left, Lisa back right.

COUNT 4
Utilized in curved follow through (Mark's right foot curving from back inward and to side, Lisa's left foot curving from front inward and to side).

COUNT 1
Mark side right, Lisa side left.

COUNT 2
Mark left together right, Lisa right together left.

COUNT 3
Mark side right, Lisa side left.

COUNT 4
Utilizes back cross follow through (Mark's left foot beginning to cross in back of right, Lisa's right foot beginning to cross back of left), partners turning into left open position.

CROSSOVER (Ctd.)

COUNT 1
Mark crosses left back of right, Lisa crosses right back of left.

COUNT 2
Mark in place right, Lisa in place left. Note: Mark begins pivoting on right foot, Lisa begins pivoting on left foot, coming into closed position (partners facing each other) at count 3.

COUNT 3
Mark side left, Lisa side right.

COUNT 4
Utilizes back cross follow through, partners moving into a close right open position.

COUNT 1
Mark crosses right behind left, Lisa crosses left behind right.

COUNT 2
Mark in place left, Lisa in place right.

COUNT 3
Mark side right, Lisa side left.

COUNT 4
Utilizes back cross follow through.

Sequence may be repeated as many times as desired, then end step as follows:

COUNT 1
Mark crosses left behind right, Lisa crosses right behind left (dancers again in left open position). Note: At end of count 1 and before count 2, mark begins to bring Lisa in front of him, pushing on her back with his right hand.

COUNT 2
Mark in place right, Lisa forward left, stepping in front of Mark, pivoting on ball of her left foot, ending in closed position.

COUNT 3
Mark forward left, Lisa back right.

COUNT 4
Utilizes curved follow through, moving into last half of basic.

CHAPTER 4

CHA-CHA

Those readers who frequented ballrooms in the early 1950s, before Bill Haley and his Comets thrust rock 'n' roll onto the airwaves and into the dancehalls, will almost instinctively add an extra "cha" to the name of this dance. "Cha-cha-cha," band-leaders would croon into the mike and dancers would pick up the rhythm with three corresponding steps, one-and-two.

In fact, the very name of this dance, another import from Cuba, almost urges the feet to pick up the rhythm. Derived from triple-time mambo, the cha-cha is one of the easiest and most fun dances to do. It enjoyed a great surge of popularity in the mid-1950s and continues as a perennial favorite. The story, perhaps apocryphal, of how this dance received its curious name, ascribes "cha-cha" to the sound produced by the heelless slippers of Caribbean islanders.

Latin Motion, described earlier in this book should be used, and you will note that in-place steps are used frequently in this dance. Cha-cha is done in a rhythm of quick, quick, quick, and split, to a dance count of 1-2-3-and-4. (Up-tempo cha-cha rhythms use less body movement—for example, less driving of the hips.)

CHA-CHA BASIC

Begin in closed position, feet together.

COUNT 1
Mark forward left, Kim back right.

COUNT 2
Mark in place right, Kim in place left.

Note: Counts 3-AND-4 should be done in chassé fashion.

COUNT 3
Mark back left, Kim forward right.

COUNT AND
Mark slightly back right, Kim slightly forward left.

COUNT 4
Mark back left, Kim forward right.

This completes first half of basic.

Second half of basic is exact reverse of first half, as:

COUNT 1
Mark back right, Kim forward left.

COUNT 2
Mark in place left, Kim in place right.

COUNT 3
Mark forward right, Kim back left.

COUNT AND
Mark forward left (do not pass other foot), Kim back right (do not pass other foot).

COUNT 4
Mark forward right, Kim back left (again, counts 3-AND-4 are done in chassé fashion).

CHA-CHA CROSSOVER

Counts 1-2-3-AND-4 utilize first half of basic.

COUNT 1
Mark back right, Kim forward left (as to begin second half of basic).

COUNT 2
Mark in place left, Kim in place right. At very end of this count, Mark begins to release right hand from Kim's back, turning approximately one-quarter turn to his right into right parallel position, where count 3 will be executed. Kim begins quarter turn to her left to execute count 3.

COUNT 3
Mark forward right, Kim forward left.

COUNT AND
Mark forward right, Kim forward left, partners in right parallel position. Counts 3-AND-4 are done in chassé fashion (chasing not passing foot).

COUNT 4
Mark forward left, Kim forward right.

COUNT 1
Mark forward left, Kim forward right. Mark leads Kim's right hand forward with his left. This lead could be straight forward or very slight diagonal down—body upright, do not bend at waist. Note extension of free arms for style.

COUNT 2
Mark in place right, beginning to pivot on ball of right foot (left shoulder back) to go through closed position, Mark's left hand pulling Kim's right hand back causing her to pivot on ball of left foot (right shoulder back) to go through closed position. Kim in place left. (Leads described count 1, 2 are repeated during reverse and repeat of crossover sequence.)

CHA-CHA CROSSOVER (Ctd.)

COUNT 3
Mark side left, Kim side right, Mark beginning to take Kim's left hand with his right hand (partners facing each other).

COUNT AND
Mark right together left, Kim left together right. Note: At this point, partners holding both hands and continuing to turn.

COUNT 4
Mark continues turning body to left, stepping forward left in left parallel position. Kim continues turning body right, stepping forward right.

Process now to be reversed, as follows:

COUNT 1
Mark forward right, Kim forward left.

COUNT 2
Mark in place left, beginning to pivot on left (right shoulder back) as to go through closed position, Kim in place right.

COUNT 3
Mark side right, Kim side left, partners facing each other, Mark taking Kim's right hand with his left.

COUNT AND
Mark left together right, Kim right together left, continuing to turn.

COUNT 4
Mark forward right in right parallel position, Kim forward left in right parallel position.

Continue sequence as many times as desired, then, to end pattern, do open turn (instructions follow). Note: More flamboyance should be achieved by greater extension of arms than it was possible to show in these photographs.

OPEN TURN (Ending in Closed Position)

This is used to come out of the crossover and many other steps. Begin from parallel position (as in crossover).

COUNT 1
Mark forward left, Kim forward right

COUNT 2
Mark in place right, beginning to pivot on right with left shoulder back, bringing Kim's right arm in downward circle with his left hand. Kim in place left, beginning to pivot on left with right shoulder back.

COUNT 3
Mark side left, Kim side right, partners facing each other. Note: Mark's left hand continuing to swing Kim's right hand in a downward circular motion. Mark beginning to take Kim's left hand with his right.

COUNT AND
Mark right together left, Kim left together right. Note: Circular arms continuing to move until hand release (Mark's left hand from Kim's right hand).

COUNT 4
Mark forward left into left parallel position, Kim forward right into left parallel position, style arms extended.

COUNT 1
Mark forward right, Kim forward left. Partners begin rolling off each other's arms. Mark turning left while pivoting on right foot half pivot to face opposite direction where count 2 will be executed. Kim turning to her right, pivoting on left foot half pivot ready to execute count 2. Partners going into apart positon (no contact).

COUNT 2
Mark forward left, Kim forward right, Mark's left hand beginning to take Kim's right hand, Mark continuing to turn, left shoulder back, pivoting on ball of left foot taking partner in closed position. Kim pivoting on right foot right shoulder back.

OPEN TURN (Ending in Closed Position) (Ctd.)

Note: Count AND, count 4, remain in closed position as in count 3.

COUNT 3
Mark right together left. Kim left together right.

COUNT AND
Mark in place left together right, Kim in place right together left.

COUNT 4
Mark in place right together left, Kim in place left together right.

Open turn may end in closed position (as illustrated) or may end in apart position by man stepping slightly away from partner on count 2 of open forward turn, thereby ending chassé rhythm 3-AND-4 facing each other but apart (as illustrated in the following sequence).

OPEN TURN (Ending in Apart Position)

Begin in left parallel position as to go into open turn.

COUNT 1
Allen forward right, Lisa forward left. partners begin rolling off arms and turning (as previously described in open turn), Allen pivoting on right foot, left shoulder back (a little less than half turn), Lisa pivoting on left foot, right shoulder back (half turn).

COUNT 2
Allen forward left, continuing to turn (left shoulder back), pivoting on ball of left foot until facing partner. Lisa forward right, continuing to turn (right shoulder back), pivoting on right until facing partner.

COUNT 3
(Partners now facing each other in apart position—no contact.) Allen right together left, Lisa left together right.

COUNT AND
Allen left together right, Lisa right together left.

COUNT 4
Allen right together left, Lisa left together right.

HALF CHASE

Begin in apart position (no contact between partners), then:

COUNT 1
Allen forward left, beginning to turn upper torso, right shoulder back, causing a pivot to occur on ball of left foot. Continue pivot until half turn has been achieved. Lisa back right.

HALF CHASE (Ctd.)

COUNT 2
Allen in place right (Note: Although Allen's count 2 is an in-place step, the dancer should think of it as a forward step to avoid a natural tendency of the leg to pull back), Lisa in place left.

COUNT 3
Allen forward left, Lisa forward right.

COUNT AND
Allen forward right, Lisa forward left. (Note: do not pass lead foot.)

COUNT 4
Allen forward left, Lisa forward right (count 3-AND-4 in forward chassé fashion).

COUNT 1
Allen forward right, Lisa forward left. At end of count 1, Allen pivoting half turn on right foot to left (left shoulder back), Lisa pivoting half turn on left foot to right (right shoulder back).

COUNT 2
Allen forward left, Lisa forward right.

HALF CHASE (Ctd.)

COUNT 3
Allen forward right, Lisa forward left.

COUNT AND
Allen forward left, Lisa forward right. (Note: do not pass lead foot.)

COUNT 4
Allen forward right, Lisa forward left. (Counts 3-AND-4 again being done in chassé fasshion.)

The Half Chase may be repeated as many times as desired. To end, Allen goes into straight basic (do *not* turn). When Lisa turns to find Allen facing her (visual lead), she begins last half of basic on following count 1 (her left foot forward). (A few basics may be done in apart position.) Allen returns to closed position during chassé portion (count 3-AND-4) of last half of basic by taking slightly larger steps.

KICK STEP

Begin in right parallel position (as in crossover), then:

COUNT 1
Allen forward left, Lisa forward right.

COUNT 2
Allen in place right, beginning to pivot on ball of right foot, left shoulder back, Lisa in place left, beginning to pivot on ball of left foot, right shoulder back.

COUNT 3
Allen side left, Lisa side right, partners facing each other, Allen taking Lisa's left hand with his right (partners now holding both hands).

COUNT AND
Allen raises right foot near left leg, Lisa raises left foot near right leg. Allen begins to raise Lisa's right arm with his left and begins to bring her left arm downward and inward with his right.

COUNT 4
Allen kicks right leg (from knee down, with arched right foot), crossing it slightly in front of left, Lisa kicks left foot slightly in front of her right in same fashion. Arms continue motion.

COUNT AND
Allen side right, beginning to raise Lisa's left hand with his right, and beginning to lower Lisa's right hand with his left. Lisa side left, partners facing each other.

KICK STEP (Ctd.)

COUNT 1

Allen brings ball of left foot near right foot (no change of weight), left knee isolation in, Lisa brings ball of right foot near left foot, right knee isolation in, arms continuing motion.

COUNT AND

Allen side left, Lisa side right, partners facing each other. Allen begins to raise Lisa's right arm with his left and begins lowering her left arm with his right.

COUNT 2

Allen brings ball of right foot near left, right knee isolation in, Lisa brings ball of her left near right, left knee isolation in, arms continuing motion.

COUNT 3

Allen begins to lower Lisa's right arm with his left and begins to raise her left arm with his right. Allen begins turning upper torso into right parallel position, continuing to move Lisa's left arm with his right until Allen's right and Lisa's left hands break away. Allen's right foot forward. Lisa beginning to turn, left shoulder back, into right parallel position. Lisa left foot forward. Note: Extend style arms.

COUNT AND
Allen's left foot moving forward toward his right foot, Lisa's right foot moving forward toward her left foot.

COUNT 4
Allen forward right, Lisa forward left. (Counts 3-AND-4 done in chassé fashion.)

This sequence may be repeated as many times as desired. To end this step, execute open turn previously described.

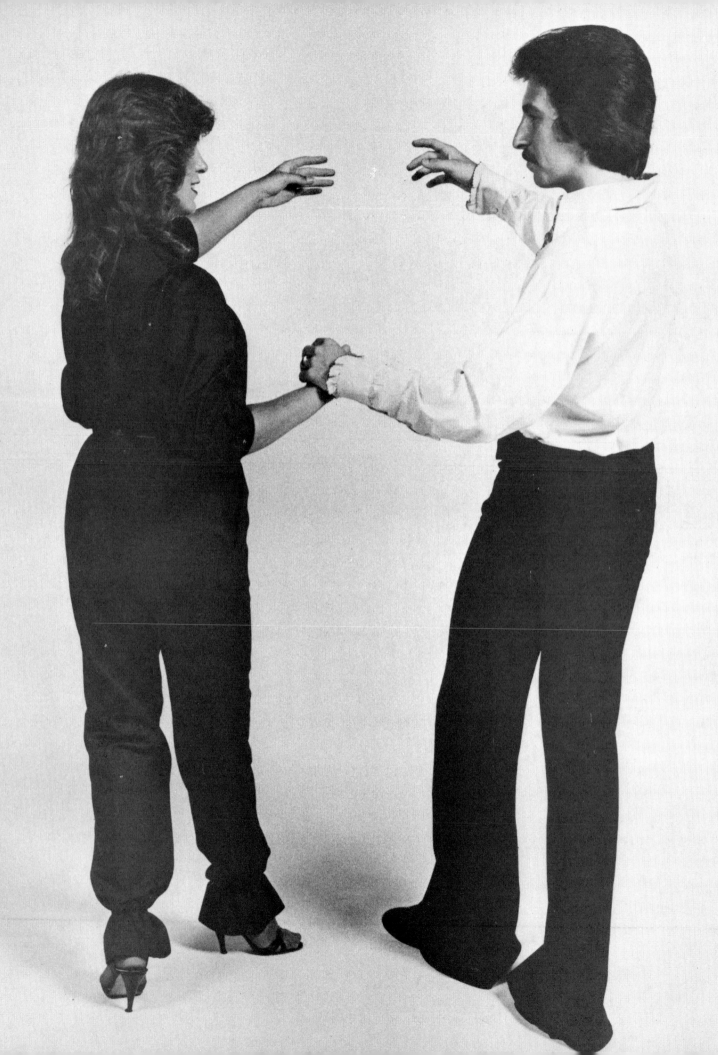

CHAPTER 5

MERENGUE

Of all the Latin dances, the lively, distinctive merengue probably is the easiest to learn. As with the cha-cha, it came into popularity in the United States in the 1950s, and is claimed to have equally colorful origins. It incorporates a "limp" step that is said to trace back to a general in the Dominican Republic whose guests thought it prudent to imitate his hobbled moves on the dance floor.

Merengue music is similar to a samba rhythm, but is less smooth, is not as melodic, and has a more driving beat. Its basic rhythm is 1-2-3-4.

This illustration is used to demonstrate the distinctive "limp" step that is characteristic of this dance. This movement is common to most third counts in this dance and creates the illusion of a limp (however, the leg is not necessarily locked and does have freedom to move). Lisa is shown here demonstrating a tilting motion from the waist, usually done by beginning dancers (during steps this tilt would be done to the right by the woman and to the left by tho man). Mark is demonstrating a rib cage movement, pulling the upper torso to the side, and a hip motion to the opposite side. This motion is used by more experienced dancers. Again, this motion would be done to the right by the women and to the left by the man.

MERENGUE BASIC

Begin in closed position.

COUNT 1
Mark side left, Lisa side right.

COUNT 2
Mark right together left, Lisa left together right.

COUNT 3
Mark side left, Lisa side right. On count 3, Mark's hip moves to right, rib cage to left; exact opposite for Lisa. (Keep in mind that beginners may use the "tilt," as described above, to simulate the rib-cage/hip movement.

COUNT 4
Mark right together left, Lisa left together right.

LEFT OPEN MERENGUE

Begin in closed position.

COUNT 1
Mark leads Lisa into left open position, stepping forward left, Lisa forward right. For a more flamboyant look, other leg may raise as supporting leg drops (with bent knee).

COUNT 2
Mark forward right, pivoting on right to begin returning to closed position, Lisa forward left, pivoting to begin returning to closed position.

COUNT 3
Mark side left, Lisa side right.

COUNT 4
Mark right together left, Lisa left together right.

MERENGUE SWING

Begin this step by doing one complete basic, counts 1-2-3-4, then:

COUNT 1
Mark back left, pushing Lisa away with his left hand, her right hand, releasing his right hand from Lisa's back, right arm moving in an upward motion (which helps to lead Lisa's arm upward). Lisa back right.

COUNT 2
Mark in place right, beginning to bring palm of right hand to Lisa's left. Lisa in place left.

COUNT 3
Mark side left, Lisa side right (keeping in mind the characteristic merengue movement which occurs on count 3). Palm of Mark's hand now pushing against Lisa's left as she pushes her left against his right.

COUNT 4
Mark in place right, Lisa in place left. Partners begin to push palms away from each other to repeat step as many times as desired. Right turn should be used while working in and away from partner.

Step ends with Mark putting arm around Lisa's waist in place of palm-to-palm. If step is to be repeated (as it should be a number of times) in a right turn, Lisa would step forward right—instead of to side—on count 3. Count 3 then would be:

COUNT 3
Mark side left, Lisa forward right.

CIRCLE STEPS

Merengue forward motion is achieved by man traveling in a straight line forward, his partner straight back. Merengue back motion would be the reverse. Remember: Count 3 movement should be applied throughout the dance.

Forward circle steps may be executed by man traveling forward on all steps in circle to left, his partner traveling back. Circle may be wide or tight, depending upon the amount of turn initiated.

Back circle steps may be achieved by man taking all back steps, woman taking all forward steps, in circle to right.

Note: Forward and back motions and circle steps also may be done with count 4 bringing feet together. This provides yet another dimension and style to the step.

CHAPTER 6

MAMBO

Mambo music, with its drums, offbeats and riffs, is a lively marriage of Latin American and jazz rhythms. It affords lots of opportunity for freestyle dancing as partners move from closed to open positions.

In the late 1940s, mambo came out of the cane fields of Cuba and into the clubs of Havana and the ballrooms of London, New York and other cities in Europe and the United States. By the 1950s, band leader Pérez Prado had become the dance's most famous advocate, helping to popularize mambo the way Xavier Cougat had the rumba.

This dance is done to single-, double- and triple-time rhythm, with single-time being the most popular. However, good dancers are able to move freely from single- to double-time. The steps detailed in this chapter utilize single-time rhythm. The basic mambo steps off on count 2, counts being 2-3-4-1 (quick-quick-slow), with count 1 being used for follow through.

MAMBO BASIC

Begin in closed position.

COUNT 1
Hold.

COUNT 2
Mark forward left, Lisa back right.

COUNT 3
Mark in place right, Lisa in place left.

COUNT 4
Mark back left, Lisa forward right. Note: This completes first half of basic. Direction in which these steps are taken is exactly the same as in the cha-cha basic—but without chassé rhythm.

Begin second half of basic, as:

COUNT 1
Utilized in back follow through for Mark, forward follow through for Lisa.

COUNT 2
Mark back right, stepping on ball of right foot as to afford a more driving motion of body on count 3, Lisa forward left. Note: In mambo as well as cha-cha, when count 2 is a back step it is almost always done in this fashion.

COUNT 3
Mark in place left, Lisa in place right.

COUNT 4
Mark forward right, Lisa back left.

CROSSOVER

Do first half of basic, 2-3-4, count 1 used for follow through, Mark's right leg swinging back, Lisa's left leg swinging forward, then:

COUNT 2
Mark back right, Lisa forward left, as to begin last half of basic.

COUNT 3
Mark in place left, Lisa in place right. At the end of count 3 Mark releases right arm from Lisa's back, turning into right parallel position. Note: Slight pivot may occur on Mark's left and Lisa's right during change of position, preparing for count 4.

COUNT 4
Mark forward right, Lisa forward left in right parallel position (arms beginning to move out and up for style).

CROSSOVER (Ctd.)

COUNT 1
Forward follow through, Mark left foot, Lisa right foot.

COUNT 2
Mark forward left, Lisa forward right, remaining in right parallel position. (For more stylish footwork dancers may step in a toe-ball-heel sequence, as to push into floor on most forward steps.)

COUNT 3
Mark in place right, Lisa in place left, starting to turn, Mark pivoting on ball of right foot, Lisa on ball of left foot (as to go through closed position), Mark's left shoulder back, Lisa's right shoulder back. Continue turn into left parallel position.

COUNT 4
Mark forward left, Lisa forward right, Mark taking Lisa's left hand with his right. Note: Do not, in steps such as crossover, release one hand until you have the other.

COUNT 1
This count utilizes forward follow through.

COUNT 2
Mark forward right, Lisa forward left.

COUNT 3
Mark in place left, beginning to pivot on left foot, turning upper torso, right shoulder back. Lisa in place right, beginning to pivot on right foot, upper torso turning left, shoulder back. Dancers continue turn through closed into right parallel position, count 4, to follow:

COUNT 4
Mark forward right, Lisa forward left.

Mambo crossover may be repeated as many times as desired and dancers would end mambo crossover the same as they ended cha-cha crossover, with open forward turn (except that mambo uses counts 2-3-4 rather than 1-2-3-and-4).

KICK STEP

Partners dance into right parallel position, as in crossover (rhythm is 2-3-4-1-and-2-and-3-4).

COUNT 2
Mark forward left, Lisa forward right.

COUNT 3
Mark in place right, beginning to pivot on right, left shoulder back, moving into closed position, Lisa in place left, beginning to pivot on left, right shoulder back, moving into closed position. Mark's right hand beginning to take Lisa's left hand.

COUNT 4
Mark side left, Lisa side right, partners holding both hands.

COUNT 1
(In this case, count 1 is used as an integral part of the step, rather than just as follow through.) Mark kicks right leg left, crossing in front of left (with foot arched), Lisa kicks left leg, crossing on front of right (with foot arched). Note: Kick step usually is done from knee down, not from hip, with foot arched and low to the floor. Also note that Mark's right arm is leading Lisa's left arm slightly down and toward center, his left arm raising Lisa's right arm slightly. This movement helps to lead Lisa into kick.

COUNT AND
Mark's right foot returns to position of previous count 4 (in place), Lisa's left foot returns to position of previous count 4 (in place).

COUNT 2
Mark tapping ball of left foot together right, left knee isolation in, Lisa tapping ball of right foot together left, right knee isolation in. Note the arm movement that helps prevent partners from changing weight on tap segment: Mark's left hand leading Lisa's right hand toward center, Mark's right hand taking Lisa's left hand slightly up and in to body.

COUNT AND
Mark side left, Lisa side right.

COUNT 3
Ball of Mark's right foot together left, right knee isolation in, ball of Lisa's left foot together right, left knee isolation in. Mark's right arm leads Lisa's left arm in toward center of body. Mark's left arm leads Lisa's left arm in toward center of body. Mark's left arm leads Lisa's right arm slightly up an into body.

COUNT 4
Mark's right hand releases Lisa's left, moving into right parallel position. Mark forward right, Lisa forward left.

You now are in position to repeat kick step as many times as desired. End kick step with open forward turn, ending in closed or apart position. If ending in apart position, you may do a half chase, as in cha-cha (using, of course, mambo rather than cha-cha rhythm)

PIVOT COMBINATION

Begin from apart position, partners facing each other.

COUNT 1
Utilized either as follow through from a previous step (with legs ending apart) or, if beginning with feet together, count would be a "hold" count.

COUNT 2
Mark forward left, beginning to pivot on ball of left foot, right shoulder back, half turn, Lisa back right.

COUNT 3
Mark in place right (Note: Although this is an in-place step, dancer should regard it as a forward step, thus avoiding the natural tendency to pull leg back after pivot), Lisa in place left.

COUNT 4
Mark left together right, Lisa forward right.

COUNT 1
Mark hold count 1, Lisa forward follow through.

COUNT AND
Mark side right, beginning to turn upper torso, twisting right, Lisa's left foot preparing to step down on forward step at count 2.

COUNT 2
Mark lunges on right foot (right knee bent, all weight over right foot), upper torso continuing to twist right, left foot lifts and extends farther to left and touches floor. Lisa forward left.

COUNT AND
Mark raises left foot, Lisa beginning to step back right.

COUNT 3
Mark stepping down on ball of left foot (in place), pivoting on left foot to left (to face partner), upper torso turning (left shoulder back), Lisa in place right.

COUNT 4
Mark right together left, Lisa back left.

Note: During Mark's part of this step, Lisa was merely doing one complete basic. This is a free-style step that may be done by either partner any time by beginning as described in Mark's part.

CHAPTER 7

SAMBA

Here is a happy, bouncy dance that is fun to do and far less exacting than other Latin American exports. In Brazil, where the Samba originated, it has virtually become the national dance. At carnival time in Rio de Janeiro, the samba really comes into its own.

Tracing its roots back to African slaves, the samba traveled from Rio to New York to debut at the 1939 World's Fair and was popularized in movies that featured Carmen Miranda (of the tongue-rolling accent and elaborate fruit-laden headwear). Following World War II, the dance was a favorite in clubs and ballrooms in Europe and the United States. The bossa nova of the 1960s is an adaptation of the samba.

Samba's basic styling has dancers leaning back on forward steps and forward on back steps. Partners also lean upper torso to the left when stepping side right and lean the upper torso to the right when stepping side left. This forward, back and side motion of the body produces a distinctive barrel-roll effect.

The dance uses a chassé rhythm (quick-and-split-1-and-2), counts 1-and-2-3-and-4. In Samba, counts 2 and/or 4 often are done sliding foot on floor.

SAMBA BASIC

Begin in closed position.

COUNT 1
Allen forward left, Lisa back right.

COUNT AND
Allen forward right, Lisa back left.

COUNT 2
Allen left together right, Lisa right together left.

This concludes first half of basic.

COUNT 3
Allen back right, Lisa forward left.

COUNT AND
Allen back left, Lisa forward right. Note: Allen leans back, Lisa leans forward, counts 1-AND-2: Allen leans forward, Lisa leans back, counts 3-AND-4.

COUNT 4
Allen right together left, Lisa left together right.

Note: Basic usually is done turning left, although it may be executed without turns.

This concludes the basic.

LEFT OPEN CHASSE

Partners complete full basic, then Allen leads Lisa into left open position. (In a "close" closed position, lead is enhanced by man raising his right elbow which, in turn, raises the woman's left elbow as well as turning hand on back.)

COUNT 1
Allen forward left, Lisa forward right.

COUNT AND
Allen forward right, Lisa forward left, as in chasse fashion (do not pass foot).

COUNT 2
Allen pulls left foot back, crossing in front of right on ball of left foot. Lisa pulls right foot back, crossing in front of left on ball of right foot. Dancers may be on balls of both feet in this position and may lean slightly forward.

COUNT 3
Allen forward right, Lisa forward left. At this count, if dancers leaned forward on count 2, they return to upright position.

COUNT AND
Allen forward left, Lisa forward right, as in chassé fashion (do not pass foot).

COUNT 4
Allen pulls right foot back, crossing in front of left, Lisa pulls left foot back, crossing in front of right, once more on balls of front feet or both feet.
Note: 1-AND-AND counts are done in relaxed but upright position (no lean); on pulling counts 2 and/or 4, body leans forward.

Left open chassé may be repeated as many times as desired. To end this step, Allen would step in place right foot count 4 (replacing count 4 above) instead of crossing, while leading Lisa with hand on back, moving her forward to cause her to step left foot in front of him (rather than her cross). Allen turns Lisa with hand on back, causing her to pivot on left foot into closed position.

Left open chassé also may be led into from crossover (instructions for crossover follow).

CROSSOVER

Begin in closed position.

COUNT 1
Allen side left, Lisa side right.

COUNT AND
Allen crosses right back of left on ball of foot, Lisa crosses left back of right on ball of foot.

COUNT 2
Allen in place left, Lisa in place right.

This completes first half of crossover, second half begins as follows:

COUNT 3
Allen side right, Lisa side left.

COUNT AND
Allen crosses left back of right on ball of foot, Lisa crosses right back of left on ball of foot.

COUNT 4
Allen in place right, Lisa in place left.

This completes last half of crossover. Crossover may be repeated as many times as desired. You may end crossover by using the ending provided for the left open chassé.

RIGHT OPEN CHASSE

Right open chassé may be led into after first half of basic or first half of crossover by man releasing his right hand from partner's back during count 2 and turning into right parallel position. We will illustrate this pattern from the crossover.

Begin in closed position.

COUNT 1
Allen side left, Lisa side right.

COUNT AND
Allen crosses right foot in back of left on ball of right foot, Lisa crosses left foot in back of right on ball of left foot.

COUNT 2
Allen in place left, beginning to pivot on ball of left foot, right shoulder back, right hand releasing from Lisa's back, beginning to turn into right parallel position. Lisa in place right, beginning to pivot on ball of right foot, left shoulder back, beginning to turn into right parallel position.

COUNT 3
Allen steps forward right (in right parallel position), Lisa forward left.

COUNT AND
Allen forward left, Lisa forward right (chassé fashion).

COUNT 4
Allen right foot pulling back crossing in front of left on ball of foot, Lisa left foot pulling back crossing in front of right. Style as in left open chassé.

COUNT 1
Allen forward left, crossing left in front of right, beginning movement into closed position, palm of Allen's right hand approaching palm of Lisa's left, Lisa forward right, crossing right in front of left, beginning to return to closed position.

COUNT AND
Allen forward right, Lisa forward left (chassé fashion). Note: At end of this count, Allen's right palm now presses against Lisa's left palm.

COUNT 2
Allen pulls left foot on ball of foot crossing in front of right, Lisa pulls right foot on ball of foot crossing in front of left.

AT END OF COUNT 2
Partners push against palms of hands, thus beginning to open once more into right parallel position.

COUNT 3 AND 4
Partners do chassé in right parallel position, Allen leading with right foot, right-left-right, Lisa leading with left foot, left-right-left.

Right open chassé may be repeated as many times as desired.

COUNT 1
To end step, instead of crossing on count 4, Allen would step forward in front of Lisa, pivoting on left foot, beginning to approach closed position, Lisa in place right.

COUNT AND
Allen back diagonal (strong left turn on left foot, bringing diagonal step more side than back), Lisa forward left.

COUNT 2
Allen pull left together right, Lisa pull right together left, into closed position.

SAMBA ROCKS

Begin with one complete samba basic, then:

COUNT AND
Allen extending left leg forward, tilting back, Allen's left hand down and pushing Lisa's right hand back. Lisa back right on ball of right foot, tilting forward.

COUNT 1
Allen in place right, Lisa in place left.

COUNT AND
Allen steps back on ball of left foot, bringing Lisa's right arm forward by pulling his left arm back, tilting body forward, Lisa forward right, tilting back.

COUNT 2
Allen in place right, Lisa in place left.

Samba rocks may be repeated as many times as desired and may be ended by going into basic.

CHAPTER 8

TANGO

Tango music conjures many images. To many, the stirring, driving rhythm of the tango is associated with one of the most sensuous, torrid dances to ever scorch a ballroom floor. To others, it represents a macho image—of Rudolf Valentino dressed as a gaucho stepping haughtily across the screen.

To the dance purist, the tango is the quintessence of high styling. Unquestionably, it is a dancer's dance, incorporating sophisticated movement and a well-developed sense of knees-bent balance. It is a dance that puts a premium on control; one in which partners truly move as one. To a ballroom purist, a well-executed tango is as satisfying as is a flawless downhill run to an Alpine skier.

Some historians claim that the tango originated as an African ceremonial dance and that it was introduced to Spain centuries ago by the Moors. The dance arrived in the United States and Europe in the early 20th century via the Caribbean and Argentina, where it had the reputation of an erotic dance performed in seedy clubs and working-class dance halls. It quickly caught on in Europe, where exponents of its sensuous dips and bends displayed their expertise at "tango teas," and in the United States where, in addition to Rudolph Valentino, it was popularized by such film luminaries as Ginger Rogers and Fred Astaire, Carole Lombard and George Raft.

The first three steps in tango dealt with in this chapter will have a rhythm of slow-slow, counts 1-2-3-4. We also will describe a tango close with a rhythm of quick-quick-slow, counts 5-6-7-8. Basic-through-intermediate dancers often tag a tango close on to most steps, as slow-slow-quick-quick-slow, counts, 1-2-3-4-5-6-7-8. Tango basic styling features bent knees and all forward motions driving from the hip—which initiates long steps. (Dancers should strive to keep hips over knees so as not to have legs extended too far in front of body.) The dance is best done with close body contact. Tango's characteristic contra-body movement also should be noted.

TANGO BASIC FORWARD MOTION

Begin in close closed position, knees bent.

COUNT 1
Allen forward left, Lisa back right. Allen's upper torso moving left shoulder back. Lisa's upper torso moving right shoulder forward (in opposition to feet).

COUNT 2
(a follow through motion) Allen's right foot in motion forward, Lisa's left foot in motion back, preparing to step on count 3. During follow through, upper torso beginning to reverse position.

COUNT 3
Allen forward right, Lisa back left, Allen's upper torso turning right shoulder back, Lisa's upper torso turning left shoulder forward.

COUNT 4
Allen balance left together right, Lisa balance right together left, bodies squared off in closed position. Note: This step ended in a balance position, Allen's left foot free ready for next step, Lisa's right foot free ready for next step.

TANGO BASIC LEFT OPEN

Begin in closed position, feet together (one foot could be in balance position, such as at end of basic forward motion just described). Allen leads Lisa into left open position, then:

COUNT 1
Allen forward left, Lisa forward right.
Note: Although dancers are stepping into left open position, in tango this is, by and large, a "close" closed left open position, i.e., shoulders do not open as they might do in non-Latin dances such as the waltz and fox trot; rather, they are more turned in to each other.

COUNT 2
Forward follow through. During count 2, Allen is leading Lisa with right hand on back, as to cause her to take next step, count 3, in front of him.

COUNT 3
Allen forward right, Lisa forward left approximately 2 to 6 inches in front of Allen's right foot. Allen continuing to lead Lisa with his right hand, causing Lisa to pivot on her left foot into closed position. Pivot would be completed on count 4. While pivoting on left foot, Lisa's right foot rides close to left.

COUNT 4
This count ends in closed position, Allen's left foot in balance together right, Lisa's right foot in balance together left, as in end of Tango Basic Forward Motion.

Let's again note that partners stand in close contact, kees bent and hips over knees—a position that would be awkward to simply stand in but one which, when incorporated into this dance movement, produces a cat-like motion. Begin basic corte in closed position, feet together. However, if moving into this step from another, partners would be in balance positions, as previously noted. Neither partner will tilt from the waist up in any direction during this step.

BASIC CORTE (Dip)

COUNT 1
Allen back left, Lisa forward right. Note: Partners do not bend knees beyond the point prescribed for closed position. In taking his step, Allen steps directly back, hips staying squared off, being careful not to turn body. Lisa steps directly forward being sure not to turn body. Lisa has total control of her weight throughout this step.

COUNT 2
Allen's body continues to move back over supporting leg (his left), Lisa continues to move forward over her supporting leg (her right). During this count Lisa's left foot turning in on ball of foot (turn out), left heel elevated and moving forward. Allen keeps right foot flat on floor.

COUNT 3
Allen pushes forward with upper part of body (initiating movement from hips), transferring weight to right foot, Allen's left heel raising and turning into body (turn out). Lisa's weight, therefore, will shift to her left foot, her left heel dropping to the floor.

COUNT 4
Allen balance left together right, Lisa balance right together left, close closed position.

TANGO FAN

Begin in closed position. Rhythm of this step is quick-quick-slow-slow-slow-slow (or any even number of slow steps).

COUNT 1
Allen forward left, Lisa back right.

COUNT 2
Allen begins to move Lisa to his right side (right side position). Allen in place right, Lisa forward diagonal left.

COUNT 3
Allen extends left foot to side, heel of left foot off floor (utilizing turn out), all weight over right foot, leading Lisa with right hand past his right side, Lisa forward right.

COUNT 4
Allen's feet remain in place. Allen leads Lisa with his right hand into left open position, Lisa pivoting on right foot, Lisa's left foot fanning floor using inside of ball of left foot (as if to describe an arc on floor), into left open position. Note: Lisa's supporting leg (her right) remains bent so as to avoid up-down movement. Fan leg in flex.

TANGO FAN (Ctd.)

COUNT 5
Allen continues to lead Lisa forward as his position remains constant, causing Lisa to step forward left. As Lisa's weight goes to left foot, Allen already is beginning to turn her into right side position, causing fan to begin, Lisa pivoting on left, her right foot fanning (describing an arc).

COUNT 6
Lisa finishes fan with right foot behind left, still on inside of ball of foot in right side position.

COUNT 7
Allen again leads Lisa to step forward right into right side position and, in the same fluid motion, begins to lead her into left open position as Lisa once again describes arc with left foot (as in count 3).

COUNT 8
Partners now in left open position.

Fan sequence may be repeated as many times as desired (count 3 through 8).

COUNT 1
To end fan sequence from left open position, as in count 8, Allen leads Lisa to step in front of him, Lisa stepping forward left foot 2 to 6 inches in front of Allen's right.

COUNT 2
Allen leads Lisa into closed position as he draws his left foot in balance position together right, Lisa pivoting on left foot, ending right foot in balance together left. Note: Lisa's ending same as tango basic left open.

TANGO CLOSE

The tango close, usually done to a rhythm of quick-quick-slow, is an element of dance that usually is tacked on to most tango steps by beginning-through-intermediate dancers. As you become more knowledgeable about and proficient in this dance you probably will find yourself making less use of the tango close—except, perhaps, at the end of a phrase of music. Begin in closed position—usually at a balance, as previously described, then:

COUNT 1
Allen forward left, Lisa back right. Partners again utilizing contra-body movement, upper torsos turning left (Allen's left shoulder back, Lisa's left shoulder back).

COUNT 2
Allen side right, upper torso tilting slightly to left, Lisa side left, upper torso tilting to right.

COUNT 3
Allen's left foot begins to slide toward right on ball of left foot, Lisa's right foot begins to slide toward her left on ball of right foot. Bodies are beginning to straighten.

COUNT 4
Allen's left foot reaches together right, still on ball of left foot in balance position, Lisa's right foot reaches together left, still on ball of right foot in balance position. Note: Dancers' feet continue to move during counts 3-4. At this point, bodies are level in closed position. In phrasing to music, more advanced dancers may use any number of counts to close.

When dancers add tango close to tango basic forward motion, they do *not* come to a balance at the end of basic. Rather, they continue count 4 in motion to step on count 1 of tango close.

When tango close is added to left open tango basic, dancers *do* come to balance at count 4; then they step out for count 1 of tango close.

To add tango close to corte dip, do *not* come to balance. Instead, leg continues to move into count 1 of tango close as is done in tango basic forward motion.

Dancers may make a combination of the first three basic tango steps described in this chapter by doing: tango basic forward motion into left open tango basic into corte (dip), coming out of corte with tango close.

TANGO ROCKS

Begin in closed position, then:

COUNT 1
Dancers turn upper torso, left shoulder back, Allen forward left (Note: Movement should precede step), Lisa back right.

COUNT 2
Allen in place right, Lisa in place left. (Dancers beginning to pull right shoulders back.)

COUNT 3
Allen back left, Lisa forward right (dancers continuing to pull right shoulders back). During count 3 dancers lift upper torso and total body raises by straightening legs.

COUNT 4
Partners hold position for beginning of count 4 and then upper torsos begin to reverse, left shoulders back.

COUNT 5
Allen back right, Lisa forward left, dancers beginning to pull left shoulders back and stepping into plié (knees bent). Note: In this portion of step, dancers are executing a twisting, untwisting, raising and lowering of body.

COUNT 6
Allen in place left (toes turned outward), Lisa in place right. Note contact of Allen's inner left leg with Lisa's outer right leg. Dancers continue turning left.

COUNT 7
Allen back diagonal right, Lisa forward left (toes turned out), dancers continuing to turn left.

COUNT 8
Repeat count 6.

COUNT 9
Repeat count 7.

COUNT 10
Repeat count 6.

Note: Allen's left foot, Lisa's right foot in counts 6 through 10 are in place but turning steps, Allen's right foot, Lisa's left foot swinging out back diagonal allowing turn to occur during these counts.

COUNT 11
Allen side right, Lisa side left.

COUNT 12
Allen's left foot together right on ball of foot as in balance or tango close position (or may be slid along floor or lifted and then tapped to floor), Lisa side together left (same motion).

CHAPTER 9

PASO DOBLE

Spain was the original home of the paso doble, a one-step that first gained popularity in Europe and the United States in the 1930s. To capture the flavor of the paso doble, dancers should project a feeling and appearance of pride—the haughty look of the matador. This is accomplished by thrusting the upper torso upward and stepping into the floor almost march-like. There is almost always an accentuation of the final beat of any movement in this dance. Another characteristic of the paso doble is a feeling of body resistance—a pushing away with hands and arms.

In this chapter we will deal with steps using, 4, 6, and 8 counts.

BASIC FORWARD MOTION

Dancers begin in closed position (styling as
described above).

COUNT 1
*Allen forward left, Lisa back right (Note: Dancers
step toe-ball-heel in march-like fashion.) Move into
count 1 with slight down-up "scooping" motion
caused by bending of supporting leg (downward,
count 1—returning up, count 2).*

COUNTS 2 THRU 7
*Dancers alternate and repeat step shown in count
1.*

COUNT 8
*Allen right together left with accentuated step,
Lisa left together right with strong emphasis to
indicate end of pattern.*

BASIC BACKWARD MOTION

Same as Basic Forward Motion—but done in reverse.

BASIC SIDE MOTION

COUNT 1
Allen side left, Lisa side right.

COUNT 2
Allen right together left, Lisa left together right.

COUNTS 3 THRU 8
Repeat counts 1 and 2. Same emphasis on count 8 as in forward and backward motion.

PUSH-AWAY

COUNT 1
Allen long step forward, stepping into plié (left knee bent), Lisa back right, Allen releasing right hand from Lisa's back, pushing her right arm and hand away with his left.

PUSH-AWAY (Ctd.)

COUNT 2
Allen begins to draw right foot to left, Lisa back left.

COUNT 3
Allen continues drawing right to left, Lisa back right (this movement is not illustrated).

COUNT 4
Allen right together left with sharp change of weight, coming up to ball of left foot, Lisa drops slightly on left foot (knee slightly bent), right leg flicking back and up off floor with turnout. Note uplifted style of rib cage and arms. Lisa sharply pulls hem of skirt upward and backward (see illustration).

COUNT 5
Allen back left, Lisa forward right (partners begin to return to closed position).

COUNT 6
Allen begins drawing right foot back to left, Lisa forward left (partners coming closer to closed position).

COUNT 7
Allen continues to draw right foot to left as he begins placing right hand on Lisa's back, continuing to move into closed position, Lisa forward right.

COUNT 8
Allen right together left, Lisa left together right (in accentuated fashion as with other counts 8 of paso doble).

FLAIR

Dancers begin in closed position, then:

COUNT 1
Allen forward left, Lisa forward right into left open position.

COUNT 2
Allen forward right, Lisa forward left, dancers still in left open position but Allen's upper torso beginning to turn right shoulder back at end of count 2.

FLAIR (Ctd.)

COUNT 3
Allen leaps side left in front of Lisa, Lisa forward right.

COUNT 4
Allen crosses right behind left on ball of right foot, leading Lisa into right side position, Lisa forward left.

COUNT 5
Allen begins pivoting on balls of both feet, Lisa forward right, still in right side position.

COUNT 6
Allen leads Lisa sharply into left open position by raising her left elbow with his right elbow and turning her with his hand on her back. Allen drops flat on right foot, coming sharply on ball of left (left knee bent). Lisa pivots on ball of right foot, right shoulder back approximately half turn, stepping back left and sharply coming to ball of right foot with right knee bent.

Note: This step can be repeated once or twice or it may be followed by a four-count break pattern, as follows:

COUNT 1
Allen forward left, Lisa forward right in left open position.

COUNT 2
Allen forward right, Lisa forward left, partners still in left open position but beginning to turn into closed position at end of count 2, Allen pivoting on ball of right foot, left shoulder back, Lisa pivoting on ball of left foot, right shoulder forward.

COUNT 3
Allen on ball of left foot, turning left knee in, Lisa on ball of right foot, turning right knee in.

COUNT 4
Allen leads Lisa sharply into left open position, still on ball of left foot but turning left knee outward, Lisa now in left open position, still high on ball of right foot but turning right knee outward.